THE TALKING HORSES OF DREAMS

POEMS BY ANTHONY WATTS

IRON PRESS

First published 1999 by IRON Press
5 Marden Terrace
Cullercoats
North Shields
Northumberland
NE30 4PD UK

Tel / Fax (0191) 253 1901

Typeset in 10pt Elan by Jack Lithgow
Printed by Peterson Printers, South Shields

© Copyright Anthony Watts 1999

Cover Design by Peter Mortimer & Michael J. Adam
Book Design by Peter Mortimer

*The book cover horse is a detail from the engraving
"The Bewitched Groom" by Hans Baldung-Grien*

ISBN 0 906228 70 0

*Trade Distribution:
Signature Book Representation
Sun House, 2 Little Peter Street
Manchester
M15 4PS
Tel: (0161) 834 8767
Fax: (0161) 834 8656
email: signatur@dircon.co.uk*

For
Stephen, Rachel, Ellie & Roz

Anthony Watts

Anthony Watts was born in 1941 in Wimbledon, South London, but finally settled in Somerset. He has lived most of his life (so far) in the Quantock village of Halford which has strong connections with the Wordsworth-Coleridge Lyrical Ballads partnership. The Quantocks have inspired much of his poetry. A burning lack of ambition to do anything but write poetry meant a failure to get to university, and work seemed equally unappealing. He finally took a job as a library assistant with Somerset County Council, and, finding it not too uncongenial, stayed. He's been there nearly 40 years. Anthony Watts was married once, has four children and four grandchildren and now enjoys a semi-solitary existence in an upstairs flat playing his small collection of musical instruments and wondering where the next poem will come from. Meantime he takes long walks in the country. This is his first full collection.

The Poems

Once 7
The Apple Picking 8
Morning Tanka 9
Today I'll be a Tractor Driver 10
An Ancient Track. 11
Water Music 12
From a Passenger Seat. 13
Sea Level. 15
Bonfire 16
Untitled. 17
Scene 17
Down the Lane 18
Fourteenth Way of Looking 18
Swan. 19
Recipe for an Elephant 20
The Horses 21
Untitled 22
Dog 23
Little Symphony for a Dead Badger. 24
Dandelions 25
Untitled 27
The Wind is Oceanic in the Elms 27
Elegies for Dead Elm 28
Untitled 30
Ivy. 31
Foliage 32
How Dylan Became Someone Else 33
A Bubble 35
The Signal. 36
Before Sunrise. 36
A Molecular Love Song. 37

Inamorato	37
Untitled	38
Nine Haiku	39
The Haunted Hearth	40
Quantoxhead	41
Unicorn Meat	42
The Uffington White Horse	43
Untitled	43
Dream Daughters	44
The Freedom of the Night	45
Tiger	46
Cutaway Christmas Card	47
The Anthropologist	48
Maia Dances	50
As the Camera Backs Off	51
Untitled	52
Safari Notes	53
The Goldfish Bowl	54
Lark	56

There was once a boy whose tongue was too big for his skull
So that he could not speak

Though the whole of dumb creation petitioned him
To be its voice
         and wherever he went
Hedgerows plucked at his sleeve, flowers pressed round him
With earnest suppliant faces like the sick,
Come to a king whose hand was said to heal.

But Creation was a fever
He could not allay

And though the pebbles in the water sang like birds
He could not transcribe their music, nor could he read
The riddles of the puddling sunlight in the wood
And when the whalehead rocks thrust up
Through the broken back of the hill to breathe the sun
He failed to fathom their blinding surfaces.

        So he rented a colour TV
        And grew adept at switching channels,
        And he bought a paper and read between the lies,
        He insured his house, his car
        And the interminable prologue to his death,
        Voted always for the lesser evil,
        And so matured, after his fashion,
        Like a tomato in a drawer.

And when
One day
He came out into the light again,
Nature had forgotten him.

But he saw his children alive and kicking in the meadow
And the trees bowed gravely down to them, and the flowers
Gazed up, their eager secrets
Trembling on their breath.

The Apple-Picking

Scaling a lichened coral skeleton
Of greygreen-powdered wood, the one above
Plucked wholeness from the air; the one below
Taught flaccid sacks to stand all knobblekneed
And elbowed, round their plundered gravity.

The best fruit, least accessible,
Like water pulled through woollens hung to dry,
Clustered the leafy hem in droplets fat
As lost green rubber balls that linger, poised
On the bubble-juggling toes of waterfalls.

But one above put planets in his palm,
Easing them out of orbit with a twist:
Pot-shotted them through hastily aligned
Segments of interbranch - while one below
Caught what he could; let the rest spank to grass.

And hatched from the tree's crown, the one above
Was King-of-the-birds, cloud-dreamer, realmer of all
The prostrate fields from Quantock to the sea:
Ten fingers and as many eager years
Clamped onto every smooth unbroken promise

Claimed with a victor's shout. The one below,
Whelmed in encroaching shade, moistened his eyes
Against the lovely torn-to-pieces sky -
And thought how time turned all his rounded dreams
To hollowy homesteads for the mushing wasps.

Morning Tanka

First light. The houses
Dream, resting long shadow-paws
On distant kerbstones.

A black cat crosses my path
With daffodils in its eyes.

Today I'll Be a Tractor Driver

for Jenna

... and hoist my sail of gulls on a green lake
of pasture - my wake
a rippling spread of sheep.

Today I'll make important men in suits
go red in the face and hoot
as I lord the lanes on my oily, rubbery steed,
processioned by solemn-faced cattle

or wear a scarf of rooks
that'll flap in the wind
as I cast my clattering nets
to trawl the seas of soil.

Mounted above my man-high wheels,
I'll be warrior of the fields
in my redrust-raggedy armour
and scimitars sheathed in dung.

I want to scale some faraway hill
like a little red mite on a loaf,
my shrunken thunder
tickling your eye more quietly than a cricket's whisper

as I churn the land into chocolate, priming the clods
for a winter coat of rainsheen, printing
the puzzles and patterns and mazes of an endless welly
in the mud of wherever I wallow

and where lit furrows rise to meet
the evening sky, I'll ride the rim of the world -
clinker-dark against the furnace, a little tug
hauling the ship of the land
to harbour
amid flames and roses.

An Ancient Track

       I turned to regard the way by which
I came out on the lane. A nettled cleft
Between one tousled hedgerow and its twin
Vanished where cataracts of bramble sealed
The shut-eyed centuries in.
                              Though they should drive
Twice daily down the lane that breaks that track,
Commuting villagers might never catch
The lonely signal of its flashing past,
Quick as a blink, between two fields of corn.

Water Music

(The Bridgwater and Taunton Canal, 1995)

The motorway is a civil war; silence
A casualty caught in the crossfire.
But I am an armistice; my flag of truce
Two white swans sedent on a field of sky.

When motorway and rail are firing bullets
At distant targets,
I mirror the pathless cloud-continuum;
I harbour the Sunday refugees from haste
On barges whose destination is simply wherever.

When the motorway yells, 'Go, go, go!'
I watch the lazy sun roll back its duvet,
Break a late-breakfast egg in the well of my mirror,
Then toss the wobbly pancakes of the dawn
On the undersides of bridges.

When the motorway runs you in and bangs you up
In a prison of speed - force-fed on a diet of lead -
I offer you gold on a silver plate:
Marsh marigolds, freshly minted under the eaves
Of the moorhen's shanty raft.

While the railway cuts a gleaming swathe through the meadows,
Lines glinting, taut with expectation
Of the sudden thunderbolt cocoon
Of racket and blur - racket and blur - racket and blur -

I pass the timelessness of day
With calm-eyed cattle, their great wingnut heads
Surmounting wire and thorn. I bend an ear
To the trickled confidentialities
Of irrigated fields. I am at peace
With the ancient silence of the summerlands.

From a Passenger Seat

For Brenda, who saved me from a thousand soakings

The rain is inseminating chaos; its vistas are engendered
On the glass: primordial, spermatozoic.

Wagging a tireless finger at the weather,
This switching stick keeps time:

Whoosh-thump whoosh of the rubber-heeled baton
Policing the windscreen; someone is cutting a demi-
Disk of visibility instantly flawed

As the rain strikes back
Pitting its moon-
Craters against eradicating steel.

A press of raindrops crowds the surging perimeter
While in the corner a coiled rope of rain
Wrestles the unrelenting rush of air;

Shimmying tadpole shapes, hatched from the welter,
Wriggle into recognition, shaky clockwork
Threading invisible traceries of grease.

The drips fan out and around the lateral curves
Of the windscreen, till the current takes them and they soar
Or plummet out of sight.

A flicked switch

Highlights a head-on collision
With a squadron of kamikazi firedrops
That swoop off, however, into the surrounding remoteness.

Rain turns to sleet

And where the rain's light spangles fell
The glass is splashed with spoor of a swift beast

As though some denizen of the invading sky
'S at large in the loping wind.

The wiper wipes:

Whoosh-thump whoosh-thump,
Blind as reason, stubborn as the heart

Establishing a steady, rainproof gaze
Out on a vanquished realm of plundering waters.

Sea-Level

Swabbing the sun's blood
Staunching the wound in the sky
The fog trawls in, an almost-kneadable mass
On a cushion of visibility
Kneehigh

Low cloud
Has cottoned-onto everything
Even the loudfaced houses are humbled down
To a modest frieze
The battlements of rising damp on the fog's wall
The trees are in a cold sweat about it. They've twigged a plot
To rob them of identity
A sapping of their silhouettes to inkless wraiths
Lost in the fog's blotter. They sob silently
Their wrung hands clutching dough

 ... While the greyfeathered fogbird
Broods
Like a body of knowledge
Over the final
Unhatchable fact of the world

Bonfire

The punk-haired goddess Fire
    is scissoring out
        the souls of the sober elements:

flaking off their chains,
    they bundle up
        the helterskelter of the air

to enter, one by one,
    oblivion, each sucking
        a last desperate cigarette.

Along the scorched rim
    she clones herself
        in tiny dancing sprites;

the smokey air is filled
    with the fatty crackle
        of her self-applause

and the bonfire
    sags, collapses
        like tenements of war.

Untitled

Tortoiseshell Butterfly, wings akimbo,
tight as a transfer to the sunbaked stone,

shuts suddenly her colouring-book, becomes
this one dark fin:

pinched face, filamental legs -
little world of struggle and soot

swept under the carpet
of her opulent wings.

Scene

a butterfly in a wedding dress
scitters distractedly along the hedgetop and
    vanishes
in a chapel of shadows

meanwhile a beetle
in a shot-silk mac
    loiters
on a leaf

Down the Lane

These nestlings sleep uneasily, their ancient
Walnut-lidded eyes screwed tight on a dream
Of drowning in their own soft-throbbing feathers

Draggle-mouthed, up-peckers-all
Breasting with eaglish pride their babyruffs ...
One day, parting the leaves, we'll find

The nest forsaken, a soft hank of hay
Wound on a spool of quiet

The small hot engines gone to arrowed song

Fourteenth Way of Looking at a Blackbird

Blackbird flows
Up to the windshaken branch
Like a blot re-entering a fountain pen

Swan

His beak's a whittled
Carrot hammered home
Under the harlequin mask and the brow's fierce pain -

His neck, a meathook
Gloved in polar velvet,
Melts and bends in the frostfire of his spirit -

With whiteness whisked
As stiff as a roast ghost,
With sudden

Wingclatter and angry admonishments
Of the flossed-up tail,
Loudly he upbraids the elements

Till (water and sky
Put firmly in their place)
He composes himself to float with a galleon's grace.

Recipe for an Elephant

Take a winged boulder, fluttering tree-high
Pour on elephant-mix, letting it roll
To the ground in slow thick columns

Tease out of restless serpent in the front
And one (more docile) at the rear
Fix bayonets before the mixture sets

Let him come to wakefulness knees first, finding his trouserlegs
Slowly, very slowly begin to trapes
In a comical slow dance

Until, with a flung cry
That rips whole branches from the constellations
He enters the clearing

Suddenly, become a god

The Horses

For Roz

Two swan-necked horses of the hills
Stood like sentinel statues where the stream began

From the quality of the stillness that surrounded them
I knew they were the talking horses of dreams

Though now they spoke only with an eloquence
Of mane and tail, saying, 'We are through with speech

And all it can achieve, finding it better
To stand just as you see us, heads bowed low
With a sorrowful wisdom and a great calm

While our tottering foals strengthen their sapling legs
Here on the bountiful hillside'

I Saw a Golden Hind on a sea of corn.
She seemed to rise up out of summery sleep
And took the field in long bounds, striding
On stalks of light - a Queen of the Mayflies, honouring
A drowsy pool.

A cool reception of quietly hustling trees
Stole her away from me - but not before
My blood, in its dark tunnels,
Had cried aloud

To be poppies about her feet.

Under the jogging sun, the dappling leaves,
Dog sniffs and savours:
He follows the fortunes and flavours
Of intrepid nose.

Beneath his paws all day, this stony drove,
Heavy with history, bounces like a trampoline.
The hills hoist him aloft on their broad shoulders to scamper and play.

Here and there, a clot of shabby sheep
Loiter beside the track:
He scatters them with his eyes, but his legs are trained
And dog pants past at heel, like a faithful old husband
Hurried along a promenade of tarts.

Birds are a better proposition, pheasants especially:
Catapulted from their lovenests among the ferns
- Full throttle, motors whirring -
They beeline for the treetops half a mile away,
While Dog pelts after (though he is bound to the earth
Even as their own swift shadows are).

Then, when you want to rest on the turf and drink the sky,
Hot straw Dog thuds like a bale across your knees
Or, stalling heavily halfway up your chest
- Wagged out, radiator boiling -
Lathers you head to shirt in dogjuice.

Then up pup and away -
Rippling like heathfire through the bracken,
He snaps the pants off passing clouds.
His ears play crazy semaphore with the wind.
Through hoops that only he can see, Dog leaps, Dog bounds,
His skyline baited with larks.

Treacleback and treaclegold flow the fires of his fur
As light of life runs flickering through all his thicknesses.
A million years of evolution are a hair
Of the tail that wags him - aeons proclaim him
Sovereign Dog.

Little Symphony for a Dead Badger

Penumbra'd in the strewn hairs of his pelt,
Black Brock lies bloodless, who a few days back
Surprised me large as life in this same spot -
Some instant taxidermist in a car
Struck out his badgerhood and beached him here:
A roadside trophy for the pale curator.

But nothing we choose to call death must be allowed
To stop the music, and a scherzo succeeds
The failing breath's adagio rallentando -
Where the panting ceased, a population
Explodes from his side, see, he is all-a-wrestle
With maggots: a perpetuum mobile.

And yet, when I resume my homeward trek,
As in a kind of coda, solid Brock
Breaks clear of insubstantiation -
Outrunning the stench as it slips from the wind's pillion,
Comes bounding along behind, winding and snuffling
Into my head: into the spectral wood.

Dandelions

1

March has recovered the sun: for months it lay buried
In Winter's skip, down among dark tree-girders
Under the plump disgorgings of old mattresses
Till mad March found it, blew off the dust and made it
Into an Easter gift for April his latest
Girl who polished it with tears and smiles

But Spring meant mischief in her tinkering fingers
The sun coughed up its works like an overwound watch

And all the fields and lanes were strewn with blazing cogs ...

2

So many solar engines ticking over

With insect industry among the crammed florets
The golden clockhands pointing

To all the time in the world

Yet with what sudden secrecy they all
Cut out

Whose ghosts are so many ...

3

 ... moonballs
Star-faceted
a fluff

Of twilight on the meadows barely clearing the dew
And each one a whole

Fleet at anchor, an airfleet
Anchored in air

For the hurricane-cheeked children desperate to know
What time it is

When time has flown

4

Wingless featherless
Under the lank and draggled ruffs
These gawky bird-things nursing
Their plucked pates
In the grass

Larkhigh

Dwindling in blue
The one plumed warrior who

Just   might   make it

Back

To the heart of the sun

Untitled

Evening

        the sun comes
out like a light

        shadows of trees
rustle to the ground like negligées

The Wind is Oceanic in the Elms ...

an anchored sea beating
the shorelessness of space: here are the shrouded
women, rooted to their knees, arms upflung

downcast, upflung again in ecstasy
of grief - wild eyes
rolling the course of their licked-out bowl of sky.

Elegies for Dead Elm

For H.B.

1

Where pastures plunge, diving like dolphins under
The foaming land -
    Look, over there
And over there: those stark treescapes -

Menace of black fins against the sky -

The sharks of winter
Surfacing
Through seas of summer green.

2

Plucked from their birds, those stricken trees
Float feather-naked on the sky;

Exhibit their neurologies
(That rook's nest is a clot on the brain)
Against the back-projection of the sky;

Are crowdark Winter's lingering stain
In midst of green July.

3

Gaunt waitresses
Past Autumns froze
In mid-disaster amongst toppling trays of leaves

Now nude as pylons
Poke crone fingers through
Loops of their unravelling ivy-sleeves.

4

These green Goliaths are all slain:
    dead on their feet, flayed,
        locked in perpetual winter, they will never

more, with outstretched arms,
    serve trays of leaves
        that twinkle in the wind like wineglasses;

or, treebones fleshed in summer foliage, scoop
    basins of air (your fingers tracing
        a pattern of idle love on a girl's cheek);

or stand immense at your elbow, a lexicon
    of gestures -
        blessing, calming, betokening;

or, putting their heads together, hatch
    a big blond cloud in the blue
        air above their venerable brows;

or rocking gently (the tall prows
    of an anchored armada)
        launch their gold across the whispering tarmac;

or mimic the facade of a leafy cathedral
    (shoulder to shoulder, a huddle of towers)
        dwarfing a field to its forecourt,

humbling the drowsy congregational herds
    to maggot-size. A microscopic foe
        has entered the field - death, like a stone, in its mandibles.

But the Oaktree is both
   a cabbage
   and
       a King

also a Kingdom
   glittering rich to the tips
   of its farflung
          feather-fostering archipelagos

It is an ogre whose bones
   are a jiggerypokery
   amongst
        vast amassed fortunes of leaves

a university
   of the earth
   and of the air
        scholared by rooks

It is a jigsaw the birds are building
   vertically
   (one, arriving late
        holds in its beak

a last lost piece of sky)

Ivy

Torsos of the damned,
Those tentacles rose
Importunate out of earth's black oven;
Baked with age,
Grown thick as loaves,
Pestled together in monstrous fossil-
Agony, they'll outcramp time
- Their grossness strapped
In tight
To the tree's meat -
Below a shining accolade of leaves.

All of hard and bitter drained
From its life's long wound,
The tree grows sweet with death.

Foliage

Long fingers wrapped in beechskin -
The magician has conjured

From under the loam cloak
From the crucible of renewal

An invisible fluttering heart -

An elevated host, hidden
But felt

By the worshippers
In the ceremonial spring sunshine.

At the moment of
Manifestation

No-one was looking

Yet suddenly -
There, in the tree's hand -

A shining miraculous trembling greenfeathered bird.

How Dylan Became Someone Else

In the days when Dylan meant Thomas, we were a clique
Of dufflecoated misfits out of grammar school.
We used to crashflop in my downstairs flat
Pretending it was a beatnik pad;
Listened to Charlie Parker and Miles Davis,
Duly despising Beatlemania.
We seldom ventured on the road -
Read Kerouac instead; thought we should smoke
Something - chose Gaulois - hash on the streets those days
Was scarce - at least in Bridgwater.

One day Hotdog came round. 'Hey, man' he said
(We called each other 'man' - remembering names
Was too exhausting) 'Hey, man, listen to this.'

We listened -
            the frail white youth on the record sleeve;
The raw shock of the voice, like a freight of coal
Dragged through the delicate portal of a flower

Like Shelley had swallowed America.

One man and his guitar - this was something new.
It matched our stance of existential bravado.
We got stoned on that first eponymous LP
And, after that, 'Freewheelin''.

With 'The times they are a-changin'' things went wrong.
A diverted stampede, the Beatle-howling girls
All changed direction. We were appalled:
This wasn't supposed to happen.
We gave up on him as soon as he went electric;
Solemnly told each other he'd 'sold out'.
Scattered now and, having sold out ourselves
(To marriage, work etc.)
We read of the comeback concert, also sold out -
But to a somewhat younger set than ours.
These are the ones who adopted our orphaned hobo,
The poet who failed to die young.

We glance at the review, feeling perhaps
A touch of wistful pride, remembering

How we discovered him first.

A Bubble

       - Who skinned the rain
To clothe this quivering jellyball of air
In iridescence and a stick-on window
Complete with washing-line and one white cloud?

Here is the crystal ship that carries
The lovers up and away beyond
The warring worlds: at touchdown it will vanish
Instantly, leaving a faint, dark stain, like a tear.

The Signal

as the castaway's dreamship hove
to the world's rim snapping
the taut elastic of his solitude -

as the long-awaited dove
to the ark returning
under a rain-bruised sky -

my love my love my love

at the field's far corner flying
the ensign of herself in a white blouse.

Before Sunrise

I wake surprised to find no trace
Of love but a heart vacant and free
As the night wind in the night's embrace -

Then, like the moon clearing a cloud or tree,
Your image slots into its place,
Flooding me utterly.

A Molecular Love Song

As the perfectly symmetrical snowflake
Performs in the blizzard
A series of crazy somersaults -

As the law-abiding irreproachable atom
Tells the tornado its business,
Is the earthquake's and the cyclone's mentor -

So shall our neatly-programmed cells,
Our coded genes,
Sing, soar together in love's perfect anarchy.

Inamorato

an angel and
a devil tend
this fire -

the heart
        sings

as it burns.

Untitled

The Sun Cools to a petal
of rose: a cobweb sustains it;

a blown leaf
lopes like a stoat across the road.

And you?

        are the ember
        in November

- a warmth I cannot touch.

Nine Haiku

Enter rook, flapping
into the light; a leaf, torn
from the shadow-tree.

Love, where are you now?
It is Autumn and the woods
are full of cellos.

Chestnut leaves: stricken
shoals of fish-shapes, clogging the
dry bed of the wood.

Are you there, my love?
A holly leaf pricks up its
every other ear.

An abacus of
lobes on weeping wires: birchtree
numbering lost days.

She is past seeking -
though the windblitzed hazel-pole
dangles a limp lamp.

Exit rook, flying
untidily: an open
book hurled at the sun.

Paper skeleton
dancing in a marzipan
flame: the birch exults.

Look, a daffodil!
But the brimstone butterfly
stirred and flew away.

The Haunted Hearth

The glass slippers have claimed her
this time for good. But the fire she tended

refuses to go out: her image
lingers - barefoot - amongst the ashes

rekindling them

unhappily ever after.

Quantoxhead

There's time enough on this gold nape of land,
In the lee of the cliff's crest,
Where a cornfield swells to catch its breath
Of extinction in a gulled plummet to pebble and sand -

Time enough to hear the sea, as it curls
Thin terraced lips of foam,
Straining with tireless outcry at the moon's leash,
Envying the wind that calls all heaven 'home'.

And there will be time enough and more to listen
To the muffled heart's dim raging in the dark
(That waits upon its own translucent weather,
Cancelling hope, hopelessness together.)

Unicorn Meat

Something upstream of me - some magical
Beast, a unicorn perhaps -
Is tasting, for the first and final
Time, mortality, Marshwater laps,
In callous ripples, the majestic horn
Slumped on its cushion of moss - a dull
Weight, too gross to be borne.

Set in the profiled skull, one staring eye
Long ceased to roll -
Reflecting now, in equine depths, only
An incomprehensible betrayal. Dumb hooves loll,
Reduced to clods: sky has reclaimed their thunder.
The jealous stars drained all
Light from the phosphorescent flanks. Half under

Choking weed, netted amongst shallow
Tricklings of the polluted source,
A chimera lies - The Hunter's arrow
Converted a divinity to horse-
Meat; the drunken bell
Of its strange heart cracked, ceased - a broken spell -

And I draw poison daily from my well.

The Uffington White Horse

I run with the planet as it spins:
My silence is the talk
Of mineral man,
The hidden man of chalk
Who will outpace his frisky skin
And landscape-vaulting eye -
White-whittled bones
As riderless as I.

Untitled

For Sue

A Blackbird sings
on the battlefield - in a waste
of bones and groans

Love comes limping after. A trace
of blood on tangled wire - a single
Budding rose. Love throws

aside his crutches - one
by one they break into
astonished leaf. An old scar flakes

from his shoulders, shouldered aside
by a tender but irrepressible unfolding
as of infant wings.

A blackbird sings.

Dream Daughters

Dream Daughters rise at crack of noon; cremate
A slice of toast; set the rice crispies hopping
And bopping all over the carpet; open doors
With their bottoms. Vitus is their patron saint.
Heedless of censure or advice,
They ponyprance the kitchen chairs until
(rearing, raring under restless thighs)
They teeter on hindlegs; the dining-hurdle
Quakes beneath a barely-tasted feast.

Dream Daughters wear their hearts upon their wrists
In plastic boxes, throbbing but intact.
They monitor the beat through stethoscopes,
Mad doctors on their fingerpopping rounds
Of the long-suffering wards.
Or glide past on their magic surfingboards,
Riding the radio waves (Stumbling, you find
Miraculously scattered in their wake,
More shoes than you ever dreamed you could afford.)
Dream Daughters dive straight for the centrefold;
Fix the incarnate Dream to the bedroom wall;
Then drape their idleness across the arms of chairs,
Dream-heavy caterpillars on the outgrown leaf ...
And though an arcane language claims their tongue,
They won't look up - won't speak when they are spoken to:
Dream Daughters have no time
For those the Dream has broken.

The Freedom of the Night

For Rachel & Kirsty

My daughter's daughter lies across my arm,
Her head a dreaming stone, her breathing calm
And steady now. Her story-laden lids
Have closed at last in sleep. The pyramids

Of books lie undisturbed. If I should take
Her gently to her room, she would not wake
And then, my duty done, I would be free
To type or take a walk or watch TV

Or catch up on some reading ... Yet I stay,
Letting my cherished leisure leak away
In contemplation of her sleeping form -
Loath to relinquish what is close and warm -

As though her beating heart were mine, as though
All paths from where I sit and hold her so
Lead to a land unpeopled, barren, cold
- Where there is nothing left for arms to hold.

Tiger

Whose uniform is firelight gashed with shadows
Whose purr is an earth-tremor
Whose snarl is a final judgement on the meek
Whose eye is the laser of death

Whose terrible beauty could not be entertained
In the land of guns and money

     Whose vengeful spectre
Stalks in the mansions of power
A possessing ghost

Shaking the sky with technocratic thunder

Tearing the throat out of innocence

Cutaway Christmas Card

The ox and the ass have strayed.

Where?

The ox is coupling furiously in the yard.
Tossing the butchers out of his brain, he
Labours for peace on earth. As for the ass,
He's gone to inform the gentiles of a plan
To clinch his own salvation.
Breathless phosphorescent banners bray:
'Rejoice in the Ass!'

The shepherds?

Were putting antifreeze in their landrovers;
Never thought to look up.
They get all the news they need on the radio.

The Magi couldn't make it?

Lacked the stamina
For the journey; squandered their gifts on ephemeral altars;
Sat all night in the desert sand, computing stars.

Joseph?

On nights: double time at the furniture factory;
Says they need the cash. And anyway
He doesn't believe in virgin births.

Mother and child alone then?

The unwitnessed birth.
Held in the sky of her gaze, He
Reaches out with human hands to clasp
An absent world - two human faces,
Each in its circle of light,
Sharing a secret: compassion
For all those gone missing
This blackest night of the year.

The Anthropologist

All day long a human tide had broken
Over the village in subtle ethnic patterns.
Now, stomachs and utensils stowed away,
The villagers broach sleep behind calm eyes.
Yet how much tidier they looked these last
Few weeks, their savage dust
Swept under the chapter headings ...
Having studied them closely season by season,

He'd formed a fairly comprehensive picture;
Analysed their complex kinship structure,
Their language, myths and what he termed their 'beliefs'
(Though they had no such word. In brief:

The way their being fused
With mountain valley river sun
Bird flower and stone.
'Animism' was the word he used.)

The air was cool, the shadows long;
Satisfaction, like a beast at rest,
Savoured the cud of fresh-cropped erudition ... but
The painted wizard slunk out of his smelly hut

           and began to dance

and he danced himself back
through the crack
of dawn through the nick
of time
and into the midnight heart of the tropic flame

and in that darkness he became
inviolate panther
prowled and spat
worlds
out of his eyes

then whirling in the furnace

his oily painted body sang
flights of stars and constellations of birds
rippling horizons of sweltering grass
the great stampede
of creation

and there too   etched in as an indulgent
afterthought
              a tiny
              bespectacled
              anthro
              polo
              gist

who scribbled
in a book.

Maia Dances

Maia dances under the sky of your lids,
The churning cauldron of blood;
Her flaming hair's the river in your veins.

Maia dances round the sun;
She scarves him in a windy mane;
He roars with delight.

Maia dances under ocean:
The Squid Dance, the Octopus Dance,
The Dance of the Anemone.

Maia is body and soul dancing in concord
(Though her wicked children carry scalpels,
Maia is water - and will not wound).

As the Camera Backs Off

      like a sated brute
From some indigestible scrag-end of debate

Leaving the talking heads, the miming faces
To swivel into silhouette and fade -

So God's long dialogue with the Soul of Man
Melts into silence.

      Somewhere beyond speech
Out of impossible blankness, a star

Shudders into being

Untitled

Let the poem be a sea-
shell:
      no matter
how delicately
marked, how
intricately wrought,
how dearly bought with labour in the small
hours of the night -
if the sea not sing
at its heart
      then better
it were not made
      at all.

Safari Notes

Today the bearers fled
taking whatever books were bequeathed me

A family of gibbons
perform linguistic feats in the branches

My digital watch went berserk
raced through a dozen matchstick puzzles
and puttered out

Couldn't find the compass
the map just came to pieces in my hands

The rain   faceless as data

Gave up marking off the days
in my diary
day and night now indistinguishable

Somewhere out there ...
                        the Lost Tribe

whose dialect I came to purify

The Goldfish Bowl

Now here's a circle of Hell
The Poet kept under his hat
Hadn't the heart to tell

I mean this goldfish bowl I'm looking at

With its single inhabitant - a packet
Of amber where the light lay sealed
Translucencies dissolving, thinning to water

This is the place the poets arrive at, one
By one - for we shall not skip retribution
Even though our fanciest fibs are as close
To the Truth as can ever be told

Not for him the solace of closed eyes
Whose lids flaked off like scurf and floated away
From the paper-and-pinwheel discs: that manic gleam

Unglossed to a dull ferocity, reflects
Hammered flat, the horror of being suspended
In midst of the unseeable

The eyewheel clicks in its cavern
Drily. The brain baulks. He makes
A snap transition to the other side of the tank and
Sticks, stunned to a transfer. But

This side, that side, it's all the same to him
And only the mute mouth goes on remembering
The old game

Um-um-umming at the glass as though it still believed
In a Word
On the tip
Of the tongue

Though the tongue long since dissolved
When the teeth fell out and there were no more words
To tell what it was to have lived
To have died

Alone
In a curved space

Lark

1

Phoenix-like, the lark breaks
Covert of death, bursting up
Through the poet's old hat:
Fellows my questing craft in a
Conspiracy of outflow, as
Though Shelley and the rest
Had never been.

2

Lark, a sputtering candlewick held
To the sun's glare,
Releases the molten body of its song -

Spreading steadily out over the landscape;
Over the broad dumb-beast-backed hills,
The stone-wall-weighted meadows; cooling at last

To an echo the sky reclaims: it is a song
That never sets or stiffens into words.

3

The lark has got the jitters;
God steps up the voltage as it climbs.

At the final intolerable point of intersection
Where pure joy converges with pure terror

The skylark
Teeters

Hysterical

A threshold's breadth from Infinity

4

Lark uncorked, unstoppable
On the steps of the sun's throne
Garbles
Its plea.

5

Trembling,

The lark
Threads
With its tongue

The eye
Of the needle.

We cannot follow
With our weight of bullion.

Though time and the world
May seem to hang

Suspended

In the ringing belljar of the air.

6

Skylark -
Absconded angel,
Truant star,

Gatecrashing broad daylight

Reeling off your tipsy liturgy like a tape at fastwind,

What silent socket of nightsky
Laments your fall

Into the world from which you climb and climb
To replace what you cannot contain

The uncontrollable pulse of heaven.

Envoi

Skylark, chivvying the sun,
Scatters an incandescent pool.
Lost to the eye, its piccolo heart
Is the measure of the sky's intensity.

A poet whittled words to fill
His quiver. He aimed at the lark's throat.
But his arrows flew wide, wide. The sky
Engulfed them. The lark's song goes on.

Acknowledgments

Acknowledgments are due to the editors of the following magazines and anthologies in which several of these poems first appeared:

Thames Poetry, Vision On, Orbis, New Hope International, Five River 1, Five River 2, The Pen Omnibus, Zenos, Icarus, Smoke, New Poetry 6 (Arts Council), New Poetry 9 (Arts Council), Poetry Nottingham, Envoi, Headlock, Doors, S.C.C. Thinking Skills Module, Green Dragon, Counterpoint, Jewels & Bincolulars, Ioxta, Writer's Voice, Sepia, Angel Exhaust, Weyfarers, Deane Perceptions, Writer's Viewpoint, Poetry for Ethiopia, Reynard, Literary Olympians 2, Crosscurrents, Outrigger, T.O.P.S.